100
A CENTURY *of* SPIRIT
1906~2006
WESTERN
KENTUCKY
UNIVERSITY

The Spirit Makes the Master

Dan Powell skateboards under the watchful eye of President Cherry. To most students and alumni, Cherry Hall represents Western, for it is probably the only building on campus in which every graduate since 1937 has attended at least one class.

Western Kentucky University
The First 100 Years

1906–2006

By

Nancy Disher Baird

Carol Crowe Carraco

Sue Lynn Stone McDaniel

Harmony House Publishers

Acknowledgements

Most of the illustrations used in this volume were taken by student photographers for the *Talisman*, *College Heights Herald* or other university publications and are part of the Kentucky Library and Museum collection. Unfortunately, many of the photographers (as well as the students in the photos) are unknown. Nevertheless, we wish to thank all who documented with their cameras Western's growth and influence. We also encourage those with photographs from their student days to place them in the Kentucky Library and Museum; the authors and readers of the next pictorial history will thank you!

To those who aided in the preparation of this history we express our deep appreciation: Kathy Barnes, Sheryl Hagan-Booth, Lowell Harrison, Corey Lamp, David Lee, Elisa McCabe, Connie Mills, Lynn Niedermeier, Gary Ransdell, Justin Rexing, Sandy Staebell, William L. Spillman, and Richard Weigel.

Book jacket photographs by Bob Skipper
Front end page photograph by Sheryl Hagan-Booth
Back end page photograph by Andrew Henderson

Published by Western Kentucky University
In conjunction with Harmony House Publishers • P.O. Box 90 • Prospect, KY 40059 • 502-228-2010
©2006 Western Kentucky University
All rights reserved.
First edition printed in China

Photographs ©2006 Western Kentucky University
All rights reserved.

Executive Editor - William Strode
Design - Robinette Creative Services

Library of Congress Control Number 2005937100
Hardcover International Standard Book Number 1-56469-137-3

The 1944 *Talisman* staff designs the school's yearbook.

Office of the President
270-745-4346
FAX: 270-745-4492

WESTERN
KENTUCKY
UNIVERSITY

The Spirit Makes the Master

Western Kentucky University
1906 College Heights Blvd #11001
Bowling Green, KY 42101-1001

January, 2006

To the proud owner of *Western Kentucky University: The First 100 Years*

Congratulations on your purchase of this wonderful pictorial history of our beloved Western Kentucky University. As an alumnus, as a husband, and as a parent and father-in-law of Western students, and as President of our great University, I'm proud of this volume just as I'm proud of the 100 years of rich history which it documents and depicts.

One of the things which I treasure most about my responsibilities is that of nurturing the unique variables which make WKU distinctive. I salute the men and women who built our traditions, the architects who created our campus presence, and the generations of faculty and students who have shaped the Western experience.

WKU is on the cusp of greatness. As we approach our second century of teaching, applied research, and engaged public service, I call on everyone in the Western family to cherish this special Centennial and to dedicate ourselves to the national prominence which is clearly on the horizon for Western. Western Kentucky is destined to become a leading American public university. I hope you enjoy your Pictorial History as much as Julie, Patrick, Matthew, Brooke, and I have enjoyed our respective volumes. I hope the works of Kentucky Librarian Nancy Baird and Historian Carol Crowe Carraco and University Archivist Sue Lynn McDaniel inspire the Western spirit within you. I am confident that the 100 years of history reflected in this book will help our current and future students understand how and why *The Spirit Makes The Master*.

Gary A. Ransdell
President

Equal Education and Employment Opportunities
Hearing Impaired Only: 270-745-53-89

Kentucky
UNBRIDLED SPIRIT

http://www.wku.edu

Department of History
270-745-3841
FAX: 270-745-2950
history@wku.edu

WESTERN
KENTUCKY
UNIVERSITY

The Spirit Makes the Master

Western Kentucky University
1 Big Red Way
Bowling Green, KY 42101-3576

With nearly two hundred illustrations and the accompanying text, three long-time members of the Western faculty present this pictorial history of Western Kentucky University during its century as a state institution and its earlier years as a private school. Their production represents frequent compromises and careful choices. From the diverse views of the editors and from the wealth of images available they have crafted a composite picture of the Hill and its people that should please most Westerners who turn its pages. They have skillfully depicted the major themes of life at Western during the past century, while giving an occasional glimpse at some unusual aspects of campus life. Some of the changes in recent years will leave the readers wondering how the founders of Western would react if suddenly confronted with the campus modes of the early twenty-first century.

Many readers will be most interested in the section that depicts their years on campus. But everyone should enjoy following the changes that have come during the past century. This is a book for Westerners to enjoy—and to return to again and again. Readers may be inspired to give more carefully identified images of Western to the Kentucky Library. Such materials will be invaluable for the editors who will do the bicentennial history of Western in 2105.

Lowell H Harrison
Professor Emeritus
Department of History

The Spirit Makes the Master

Internet URL: http://www.wku.edu

THE EARLY YEARS

He earned tuition by cutting hickory trees and in January 1886, with $72 in his pocket, Henry Hardin Cherry walked to Bowling Green "through more than fourteen inches of snow" to enter a small college that trained teachers. When debts and decreasing enrollment threatened its closure a few years later, Cherry and his brother Thomas C. purchased the ailing school, renamed it the Bowling Green Business College and Literary Institute, added teacher-training courses and began a promotional campaign that within seven years increased the student body from less than 30 to more than 700.

In 1899 Henry bought his brother's share of the school and changed its name to Southern Normal School and Bowling Green Business College. Thus commenced H. H. Cherry's amazing career and the beginning of Western Kentucky University. During the three decades he served as Western's president, the school grew from a business and normal school to a degree-granting college. Although enrollment did not increase significantly, the institution's academic offerings mushroomed and the hilltop's physical plant expanded from a couple of facilities to ten major new structures, most of which are still in use.

Cherry's portrait by Sophonisba Hergesheimer hangs in the main gallery of the Kentucky Library and Museum.

Using imaginative and effective promotion and publicity, the Cherry brothers created a school that served more than 1500 students on a campus containing a castle-like classroom building, a small science building and three residence halls, the most modern of which offered hot and cold running water for the wash basins!

The school faced constant financial problems. Consequently, when the Kentucky legislature began talking about creating state supported normal schools, Cherry lobbied for one. The solons accepted and named Richmond and Bowling Green as their locations. The governor appointed a board of regents for each and those for the western school selected Henry Hardin Cherry as president. Western Kentucky State Normal School began classes in the normal school structure in January 1907.

The first student to enroll at Western Kentucky State Normal School was Herman Lee Donovan, who later served as president of Eastern Kentucky University (1928–41) and of the University of Kentucky (1941–56).

POTTER COLLEGE.

In the summer of 1909 Western's regents purchased the campus of the Pleasant J. Potter College for Young Ladies. A boarding school on the southern edge of town, its park-like campus included a three-story brick classroom and dormitory building (not quite as large as the drawing indicates) and an impressive stone home for the president. The main structure, remodeled and renamed Recitation Hall, became Western's library, teacher-training school and classroom building.

n for the Campus of the
NORMAL SCHOOL in the Western District
of KENTUCKY
at BOWLING GREEN Ky.

Henry Wright - Landscape Architect
554 Frisco Bldg.   St Louis
Messrs. Geo E. Kessler & Co. } Consulting
Kansas City. St Louis } Landscape Architects
Mr. Brinton B. Davis - Architect.

Drawing by Henry Wright

On acquiring the Potter campus, President Cherry asked Louisville architect Brinton B. Davis and St. Louis landscape architect Henry Wright to create a master plan for the new school. Although only the Administration Building was constructed, Western nevertheless developed somewhat as the three envisioned. Davis designed most of the structures built during Western's first three decades.

Before President Cherry could move the normal school to its new home, additional accommodations were needed. For about $125,000 he built an impressive brick and limestone Administration Building. On seeing it for the first time a student declared it surely was the biggest building in the world!

Recitation Hall.

Cabell Hall.

The large auditorium of the Administration Building (renamed Van Meter Hall) opened for chapel two days after Western moved into its new home. For many years the auditorium served as the site of daily chapel and as a concert and lecture hall for such well-known guests as statesman William Jennings Bryan, union leader Eugene Debs, aviatrix Amelia Earhart and Metropolitan Opera star Helen Traubel.

On February 4, 1911 students and faculty literally moved Western to its hilltop home. Gordon Wilson [English] recalled that he left his sick bed to help carry "a two horse load" of library books "from down in the valley to the top of the hill." Wilson also remembered that 15th Street (on which the new campus fronted) was then a "gullied path where even a cow would have had unsure footing." The Bowling Green Business College remained at the downtown campus and did not become part of Western until 1963.

Administration Building.

STUDENTS ON THEIR WAY TO
CHAPEL EXERCISES,
WESTERN KENTUCKY
STATE NORMAL SCHOOL,
BOWLING GREEN, KENTUCKY.

Campus Clean-up Day began shortly after Western moved up the hill. The event brought students and faculty together for work and play (pictured here behind Recitation Hall), created conviviality, fostered a sense of ownership and kept down the cost of maintenance.

Dressed in their finery, Adair County's teachers and administrators posed on the porch of Cabell Hall in 1913. Each had completed the courses for an Elementary, Intermediate or Advanced Certificate. Western began granting college degrees in 1924.

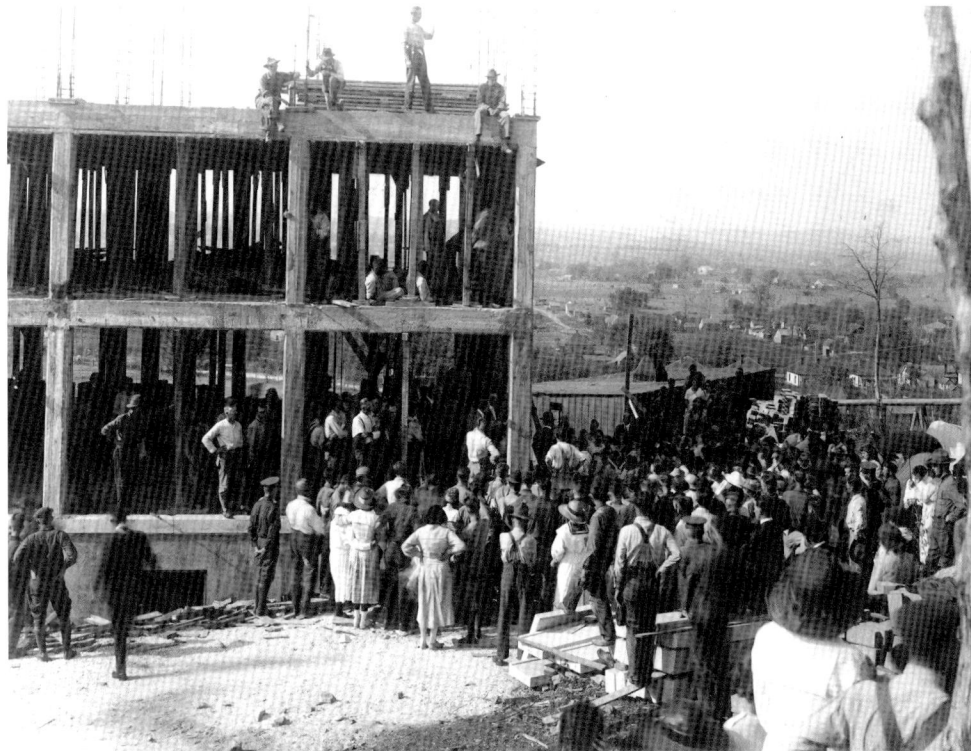

In October 1920, Western laid the cornerstone of its first hilltop dormitory, J. Whit Potter Hall. The completed dorm accommodated 250 women in bedrooms furnished with two Murphy beds and a daybed. Homes in the African American community of Jonesville dot the area south of the new building.

Photo by Eugene Franklin

Throughout the prewar years, students served as waiters in Potter Hall's cafeteria. A senior presided at each table to make sure that the diners said the blessing and used proper table manners.

Photo by Eugene Franklin

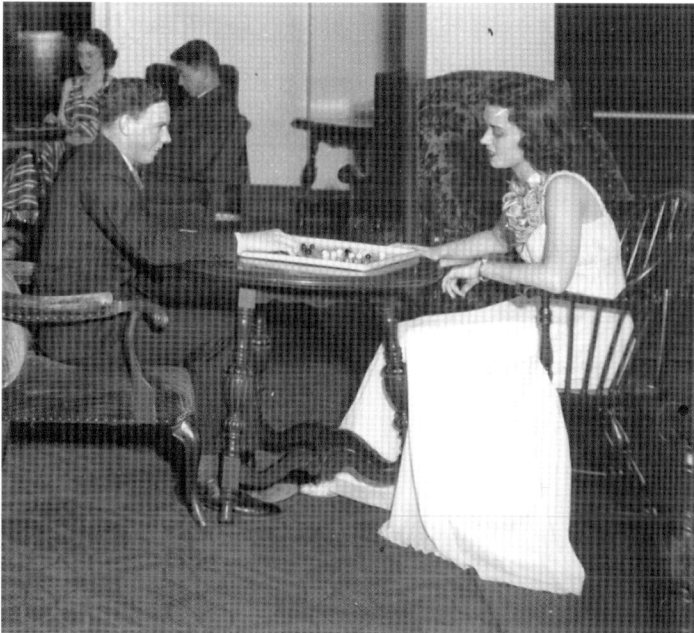

Western's second hilltop home for women (West Hall, renamed White Stone Hall and then Florence Schneider Hall) featured an elegantly furnished lobby.

Hilltop Home

Students needed a place to relax and someone suggested building a senior house with dead cedars that dotted the hilltop. L.Y. Lancaster |biology| chopped down the first tree and showed the student "construction crew" how to hew logs. William J. Craig |chemistry|, George Page |physics| and Henry Yarbrough |math| supervised the labor. Because President Cherry announced that everyone should help, Nelle Gooch Travelstead |music| and her two small sons helped cart away the remaining tons of wood chips.

Opened in 1921 the Cedar House became a student hangout as well as a showplace for dinner parties and receptions. Between 1923 and 1928 it housed Western's library. Following the completion of a new library, the Cedar House again served as a student center.

The annual student visit to Mammoth Cave was an exciting event. Memorable indeed were the boat trip on the Barren and Green rivers, train ride to the entrance, and squeezing through the cave's Fat Man's Misery. A former student recalled that they "had to push, pull and tug" to get Franz Strahm [music] through the narrow passageway.

Not all students spent their free time in the dorms or the Cedar House. After seeing a number of shrubs quivering in the moonlight, Alfred L. Crabb [education] inquired about evening activities on campus. Someone explained, "If you want to stop the boys and girls from sitting under bushes and hugging one another, you're gonna' have to raise an armless generation."

The Model Rural School, built in the mid 1920s, prepared Western students to teach in country schools. The structure was razed in 1957.

Model Schools

College High

The Training School's "College High" students, shown here with Ruth Hines Temple [art] preparing scenery for a stage play, enjoyed all the amenities offered by Western. College High graduated its last class in 1970.

Western operated two model schools during its first half century. The Training School building (K–12) opened in 1925 and offered large classrooms, indoor and outdoor playgrounds and a large gymnasium that also became the home court for Western's basketball team.

Women's intercollegiate basketball began in 1915 and although men's teams attracted more attention, the women were "fair and sweet and hard to beat." Two years before the state discontinued women's competitive basketball, Elizabeth Dabbs and her team captured the 1928 Kentucky Independent Collegiate Championship.

Although they used the local "Y," Western's students needed an on-campus gym. Short of funds and also reluctant to spend money on athletics, President Cherry called for a temporary structure built by students with lumber "that does not have to be of the very best." Western's famed coach of 42 years, E. A. Diddle, began his career in this drafty barn. "When we moved to the Training School [gym]" he recalled later, "my boys were scared to death it looked so big." The Red Barn was demolished in the early 1930s.

Photo by Eugene Franklin

The Red Barn and Training School gym proved inadequate and in 1931 the school opened the Health and Physical Education Building. Constructed of Warren County limestone and sporting a handsome terra cotta frieze of Olympic athletes, the structure's 4500-seat gym was a "death canyon" for visiting teams.

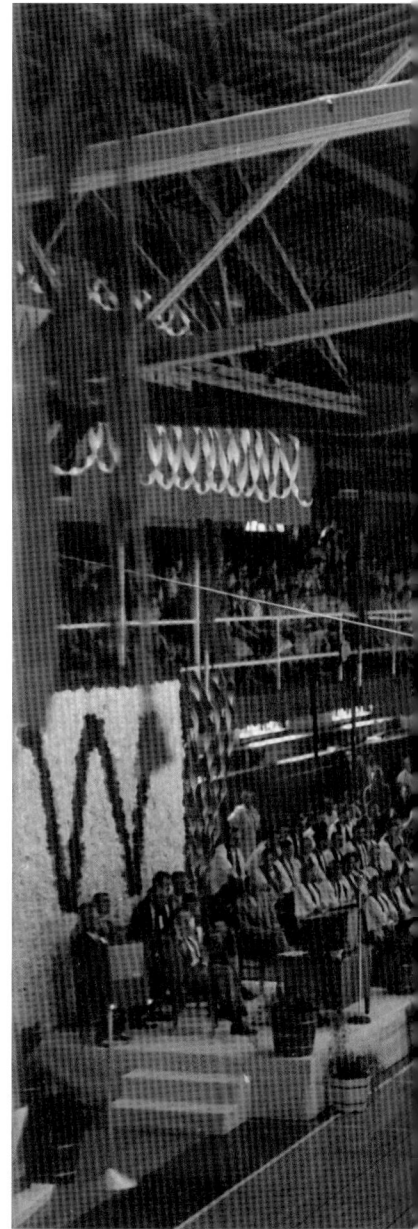

Large crowds watched Western win 336 of the 374 games it played in the Health and Physical Education Building. A coach whose teams never won at Western described his frustration: "They throw that ball up at center, the band plays Dixie and all hell breaks loose."

The Health and Physical Education Building hosted a variety of non-university activities intended as public service—and ultimately as an aid to student recruitment.

"... the band plays Dixie and all hell breaks loose."

In 1927 Western's team took the field at a new stadium in the former limestone quarry on the hill's southern slope. Having spent an "extravagant" amount to build the 155-foot colonnade and install bleachers, the regents economized by using unpaid student labor to sod the field.

"Only a few of 'em"

YEA WESTERN! ONLY A FEW OF'EM

DLETT "CY" WILLIAMS "BU
RHEAD" VAUGHN CURLY ELLIS STANSBERRY ROSS REY... DICK TYLER WICKER CUMMINS FIRPO ELROD CONN... HORSEMEAT TAYLOR "TERRABE TERRY" BALDWIN CAPT. TOM ELL...

Photo by Herman Lowe

Ed Stansbury and his teammates were among the first to play in Western's new stadium.

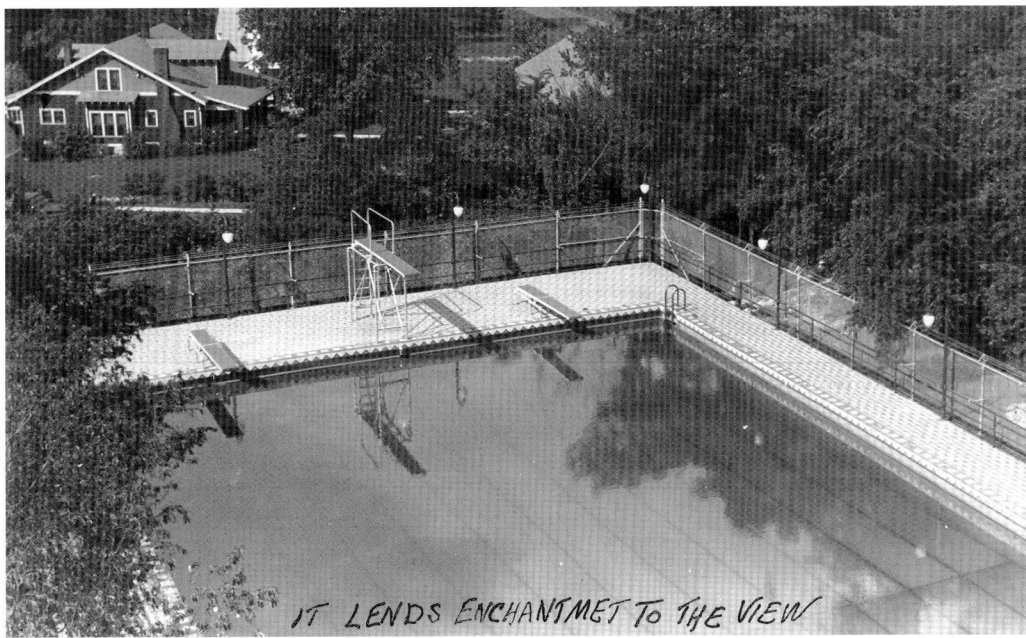

IT LENDS ENCHANTMET TO THE VIEW

An outdoor swimming pool, probably Bowling Green's first, opened in the early 1930s adjacent to the Health and Physical Education Building.

Photo by Eugene Franklin

Incorporated in 1923 to create a fund for student loans and scholarships, the College Heights Foundation operated for many years in a small structure between Recitation Hall and the Training School. From the former dairy creamery, the foundation raised hundreds of thousands of dollars and helped students finance their education.

Despite an earlier addition of a circular slide fire escape, in the mid 1930s inspectors determined that Recitation Hall was a fire hazard. Using WPA funds and salvaged bricks for interior walls, Western built Cherry Hall to replace it as the school's major classroom building.

President Cherry never wasted a penny—or a piece of building material. With salvaged materials Western also constructed portions of the Home Economics Building (1927) and Music Building (1937).

Taking care that the stone ashlars could be reused, workmen tore down Cabell Hall in 1926 and on the site built a library (later named Gordon Wilson Hall), described by a contemporary as "the most beautiful and best equipped in the South."

The Domestic Science department required that all majors live for a semester in the Home Management House. Note the fine china, crystal and flátware, as well as the relatively formal clothing of these 1930s students.

Photo by Eugene Franklin

The 1929 summer term included studies in geography and botany during trips by "deluxe motorbus" to the Western Kentucky Coal Fields and to the Rocky Mountains. Participants camped in state and national parks and stopped once a week at hotels to bathe and do laundry.

Photo by Eugene Franklin

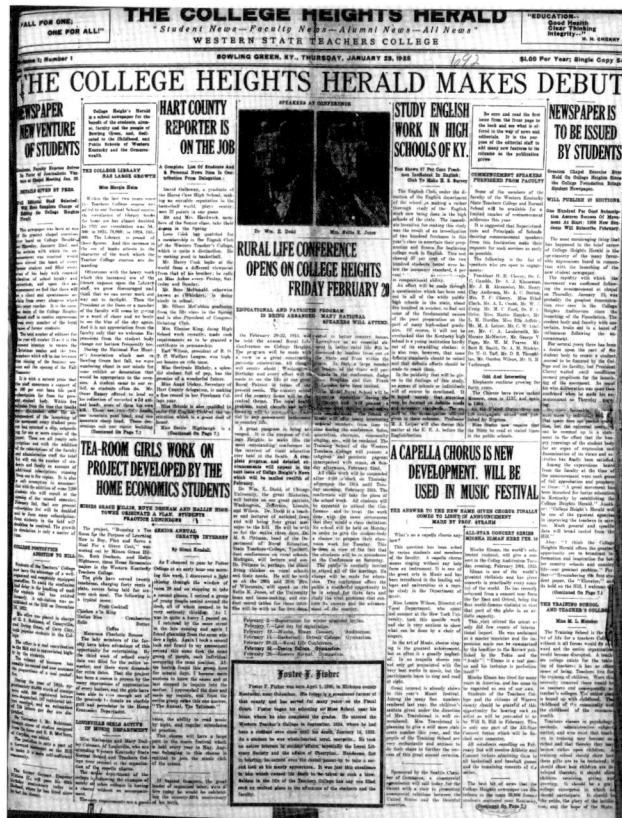

The *College Heights Herald* made its debut in January 1925. By 1930 the *Herald* was recognized as the state's best college newspaper and similar accolades have continued.

In the mid 1930s Western purchased its first photocopier for registrar E.H. Canon and stenographers Etta Runner and Ruth Tuck.

Photo by Eugene Franklin

Following its 1937 dedication, the local press predicted that Cherry Hall would be a "constant reminder of the greatness achieved by a country boy who came to his honored position from a modest little home in the hills of Kentucky."

Appearing in the school's logo, seal and other symbols, Cherry Hall's cupola contains 75 bell chimes and a carillon (added in 1974) that serenade the campus and community. For more than thirty years Claude Rose [music] played the chimes for Homecoming, New Year's Day, VE Day and other special occasions on a desk-size keyboard.

Life size bas-relief panels depicting the arts and sciences enhance the exterior of Cherry Hall.

In front of Cherry Hall stands a larger-than-life bronze statue of President Cherry (receiving final touches here by a foundry workman), modeled by renowned American sculptor Lorado Taft. Unfortunately, neither Cherry nor Taft lived to see the dedication of the building and statue.

The "Pioneer Cabin," built in the mid 1930s of poplar logs "taken from the hills near the birthplace of H. H. Cherry" and surrounded by gorgeous gardens, has served a multitude of uses. The two-room structure has been a home for faculty (including the family of film producer John Carpenter), students and visitors as well as for the College Heights Foundation, Alumni Center and the Folk Studies programs.

The Kentucky Library and Museum houses a nationally significant collection of historic artifacts, books, and manuscripts that attracts visitors of all ages and interests.

Built to house "all that is good and fine" about the commonwealth, the Kentucky Building (Kentucky Library and Museum) opened in 1939. On the surrounding grounds "First Lady" Virginia Garrett, Florence Ragland [library] and Elizabeth Woods [grounds assistant] created magnificent gardens of indigenous trees and flowers.

Western's "distance learning" efforts began in the 1930s with broadcasts from Van Meter Hall and the Kentucky Building. Library and museum staff members Elizabeth Coombs, Mary Leiper Moore and Gayle Carver discuss the commonwealth's past with WLBJ announcer Bill Kuznitsof.

No. 645

Photo by Eugene Franklin

The War and Postwar Years

America's entry into World War II profoundly affected Western. Many students and faculty marched off to war or dropped out of school to work on the farms and in the war plants. As numbers decreased, dorms and classrooms sat empty, salaries lagged and faculty members answered calls to other institutions. President Paul Garrett (1937–1955) feared that Western might be forced to close.

In the spring of 1943 the military sent 400 preflight trainees to Bowling Green for instructional programs and during their fourteen months on campus they bunked and took their meals in the two dormitories previously occupied by young ladies; the women found housing with families in town. The military compensated Western for teaching, housing and feeding the students, and the young men enlivened the social life on campus as well as enjoyed their days at the college. "I wonder if they realize how lucky they are to be at Western," wrote a fellow stationed in North Africa. He knew his khaki-clad friends would give "almost anything to swap places" with men stationed at Western.

During the war Frances Richards [English and journalism] wrote letters to many Western students in the armed forces. And "you *had* to write back!" a former student recalled. Richards kept the letters sent to her. Now part of the Kentucky Library and Museum's collection, they help provide researchers with a keen understanding of the conflict.

At the war's end many took advantage of the GI Bill and enrollment rose from the wartime low of less than 500 to 1,430 in the fall of 1946, to 1,975 in the fall of 1955. By the autumn of 1960 Western ranked second among Kentucky's state schools with more than 3,500 students. In the next five years Western's student body doubled. More classrooms, more residence halls and more auxiliary structures were needed. In the three decades following World War II, Western built 15 dorms, 10 classroom buildings and 10 auxiliary structures and remodeled or enlarged others. In 1955 the school valued its 20 major structures at about $10 million; two decades later Western's 41 major buildings were valued at $35 million.

Three presidents guided Western during the war and postwar decades—Paul L. Garrett (1937–1955), Kelly Thompson (1955–1969) and Dero Downing (1969–1979).

Organized in the mid 1920s, Western's marching band enlivened ballgames in the 1930s and patriotic endeavors during the war. In 1942 it welcomed home the basketball team following its Madison Square Garden victory in the semifinals of the prestigious National Invitational Tournament (NIT).

Western opened its doors to Army Air Corps preflight students in 1943. The trainees soon learned that flying techniques and classes in physics, math and geography had to be augmented by "Ironing 100."

Vets' Village

To aid the postwar enrollment boom and provide for the new phenomenon of married students, Western used surplus military trailers to create Vets' Village on the southern edge of campus. Residents paid $18 a month for their cramped and spartan quarters.

In 1947 Western probably was the nation's only school whose cheerleading squad boasted two sets of twins. At the 1948 NIT the Cook twins received a standing ovation following their halftime song-and-dance performance. Back L–R: J. H. Cowles, Helen Willett, Hazel Willett, Jody Baxter. Front: Anna Jo Cook, Martha Shacklette, Betty Jo Cook.

All-American

Competitive athletics became more popular than ever after the war. Coach Diddle's 1947–48 team (which included five All-Americans) placed third in the NIT.

ART SPOELSTRA, 6'9" CENTER, LED THE NATION LAST YEAR IN PERCENTAGE OF FIELD GOALS MADE WITH AN AMAZING AVERAGE OF 51.9% — HE SCORED 484 POINTS

484 POINTS — BONG

WESTERN KENTUCKY

ART SPOELSTRA

NOTHING TO IT!

S. BISHOP

TOM MARSHALL

TOM MARSHALL, 6'4" FORWARD, AVERAGED 19 POINTS PER GAME LAST YEAR, AND WAS 5TH. IN THE IN THE NATION IN PERCENTAGE OF FIELD GOALS MADE. HE EMPLOYS EVERY STYLE OF SHOOTING AND EVERY TYPE OF SHOT

A large new student center opened in 1953. Named for President Garrett, it offered game and meeting rooms, study areas, a cafeteria, snack bar and an auditorium that seated 350. Fifteen years later, additions doubled the building's size. Note the wallpaper!

Middle Tennessee State University photo by Fox & White

The Hilltoppers (Billy Vaughn, Don McGuire, Jimmy Sacca and Seymour Spiegelman) appeared on the Ed Sullivan and Perry Como shows to publicize their recording of "Trying." Their fans also remember them for "P.S. I Love You," "Marianne" and other Billboard hits.

Eateries like the Goal Post, University Inn and the Quonset Hut attracted students who wished to catch a snack, listen to music or merely "hang out." In the latter, the famed Hilltoppers crooned an early performance for a Business University dance.

Wartime exigencies curtailed many activities, most of which quickly regained their popular role in peacetime homecoming festivities. Tires had been previously rationed and almost impossible to obtain, but by the 1950s students had "tires to burn."

45

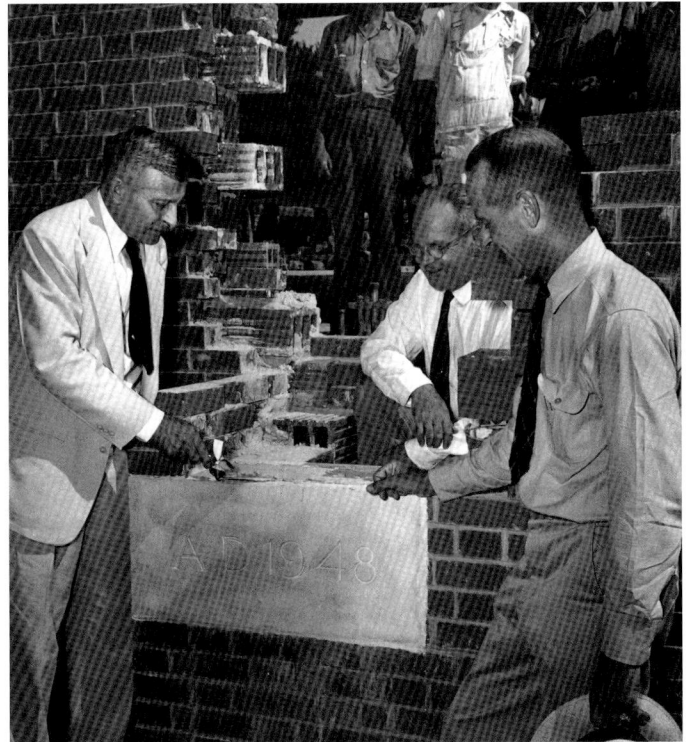

President Garrett laid the cornerstone for a new dormitory in 1948 and began an ambitious postwar building program. Through the decades McLean Hall housed more than 15,000 women—and remained virtually unchanged until renovated in 2001.

To address the rapidly escalating need for housing, Western constructed five dormitories during the 1950s— West and Regents (Bates-Runner) for women; East, South and North halls for men. The 1960s saw the completion of the six-story State Hall (McCormack), the first dorm to have an elevator; the eleven-story Central Hall (Minton); Bemis Lawrence; Terrace (Gilbert); Rodes-Harlin; Barnes-Campbell; Douglas Keen; and Hugh Poland halls. The twenty-seven-story Pearce-Ford Tower (PFT) was completed in 1971.

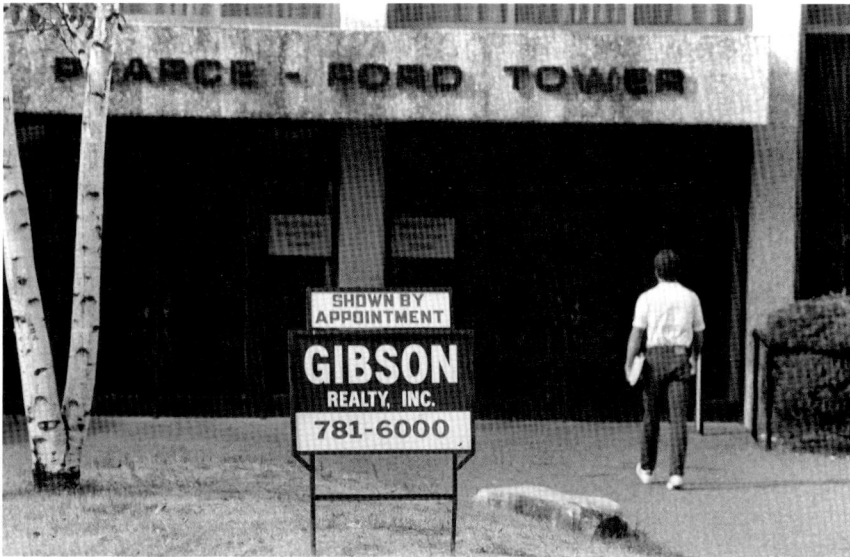

Photo by Ray Thomas

PFT is southern Kentucky's second tallest structure (only the Jefferson Davis Monument is taller). From its snack bar on the top floor, one has a magnificent view of the countryside. On at least one occasion, appreciative student pranksters tried to promote the dorm's advantages!

Photo by the *Courier Journal and Louisville Times*

More students necessitated additional classroom space. A new science complex, named for President Thompson, opened in 1961 to replace the almost 100 year-old Ogden Hall.

In the mid 1960s the Thompson Complex was enlarged with two multi-story wings and a planetarium.

"Into another world"

Named for President and Mrs. Thompson's son who died during his student days at Western, Hardin Planetarium carries visitors "into another world." Programs that provide close-up views of the solar system are traditional favorites.

Western, 1965. L–R & Top–Bottom: 1) Van Meter, the water tower, Cherry Hall cupola. 2) Potter Hall, the Colonnade, Garrett Student Center, roof of the Health and Physical Education Building. 3) roof of the President's Home, McLean Hall, Grise Hall under construction. 4) North Hall and East Hall

In 1960 Lt. Governor Wilson Wyatt attended a game in the old gym that overflowed with a mass of humanity. The building "rose 18 inches from its wall bearings as deafening applause" followed each basket, he reported. Western needed a new gym. The following year a bulldozer filled with school and state dignitaries churned across the turf to break ground for an arena of 8,500 permanent seats and space for another 4,000 on portable bleachers.

Photo by Tommy Hughes

Constructed of more than 500 tons of structural steel, Diddle Arena has a unique bicycle roof of trusses and cables to form spokes and eliminate the need for a center support. As the arena neared completion, "chicken little"-type projections circulated that the roof might fall in. However, despite forty years of raise-the-roof cheers by Western fans, it has remained secure. Coach Diddle sits beneath the bicycle wheel roof.

"Chicken Little"

Western holds an impressive postseason record. En route to the 1971 Final Four, Western defeated the University of Kentucky, a joyful victory for WKU!

A joyful victory for WKU!

Student athletes helped smooth the integration process, begun at Western a few years after the U.S. Supreme Court invalidated Kentucky's Day Law. The 1966–67 Ohio Valley Conference championship team included L–R: Clem Haskins, Wayne Chapman, Dwight Smith, Butch Kaufman and Greg Smith.

Thanks to Title IX, women returned to collegiate competition in the fall of 1973 after more than a forty-year absence and got off to a slow start with inexpensive uniforms and few fans.

"Brawn into brain"

When Western announced plans to convert its thirty-year-old physical education building into a library, students joked about making "brawn into brain." Nevertheless, the area that once seated thousands of screaming basketball fans became two-story book stacks to house the library's 160,000 (and growing) collection. Carpet covers the hardwood playing-floor, but the center jump circle can be seen in the reference area.

Construction began in 1967 for a new stadium that would seat 19,000. Completed the following summer and named for L.T. Smith [physical education], the structure offered 12 classrooms, 26 faculty offices, modern showers, and a training facility, as well as a track and playing field with a pop-up sprinkler system.

State-of-the-art

Occasionally the marching band has included non-students. Jan Weaver's dog learned a drill and became part of the "Whistler's Dog" halftime field show.

Labeled a "high stepping syncopated study in liquid rhythm," drum major Jim Simpson, the Silver Girls and the 1973 marching band are remembered for their nationally televised halftime performance at the Grantland Rice Bowl.

The new stadium had a state-of-the-art press box and provided every spectator with an unobstructed view. But at least one alum complained that fans had moved from a stadium where they "stared into the sun during the fourth quarter to one where they squint into the sun for all four."

Homecoming queen has always been a coveted honor. In 1949 Teddy Lou Johnson became Western's first homecoming queen; in 1972 students elected Alice Gatewood as the first African American so honored.

Homecoming Queens

College dances—be they Homecoming, Talisman or a Military Ball—were formal affairs during the 1950s and 60s. However, by the time Terry McGehee, Debbie Hale, Marcella Williams and Walter Taylor attended this dance in the 1970s, styles in clothing and dance had changed.

Photo by Tommy Hughes

. . . be they Homecoming, Talisman or a Military Ball

Photo by Lewis Gardner

As the campus spread southward, the need for a student center close to classrooms and living quarters became paramount. Opened in 1970, the new Downing University Center—DUC—offered bowling lanes; ping-pong, billiard and meeting rooms; a bookstore, snack bar, cafeteria and post office; and a 700-seat theatre. But its most eye-catching features were the lobby's two freestanding circular staircases and "conversation pits."

Few students brought cars to campus during the school's first half century. However, as enrollment increased in the postwar years so did the problems of where to park. In 1970 Western built a seven-story, 1000-car parking structure, but the new structure only solved the problem temporarily.

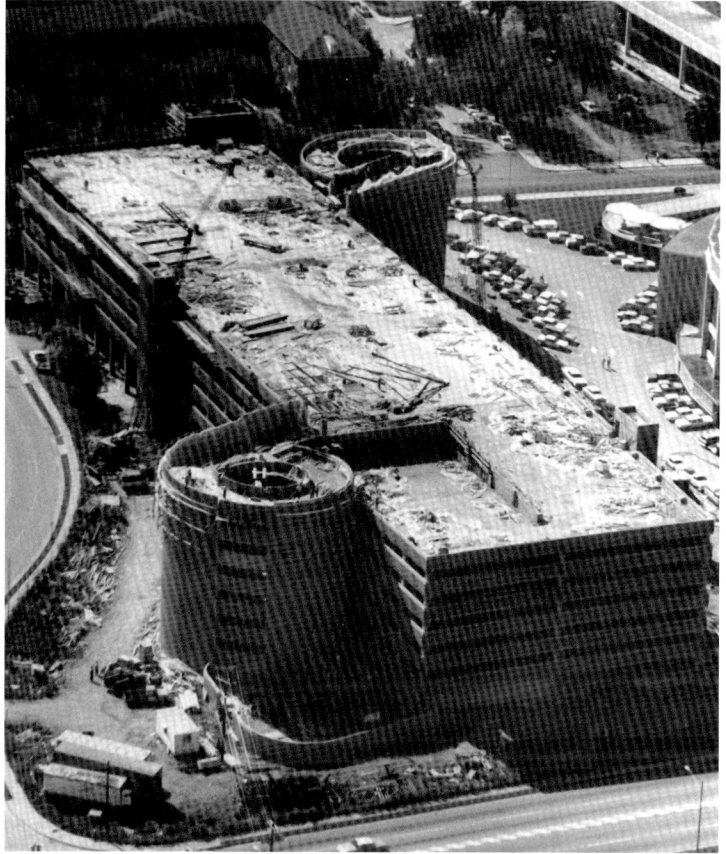

The 20-foot pylon erected as part of Western's 50th anniversary celebration announced that at Western Kentucky State College, "The Spirit Makes the Master." In 1966, when Western achieved university status, the name was updated.

"The Spirit Makes the Master"

Photo by David Gibbons

The affiliation of local clubs with national fraternities and sororities began in the early 1960s. Eventually, most of them became house owners. But whether in a frat house or dorm, student rooms have a charm of their own.

QUIET HOURS
SUNDAY THROUGH
7:00 P.M. - 8:00

Photo by Todd Buchanan

"Mice and men"

The psychology lab is a place where "mice and men" learn about behavior. The little fellow's "teacher" is Jon Theuerkauf.

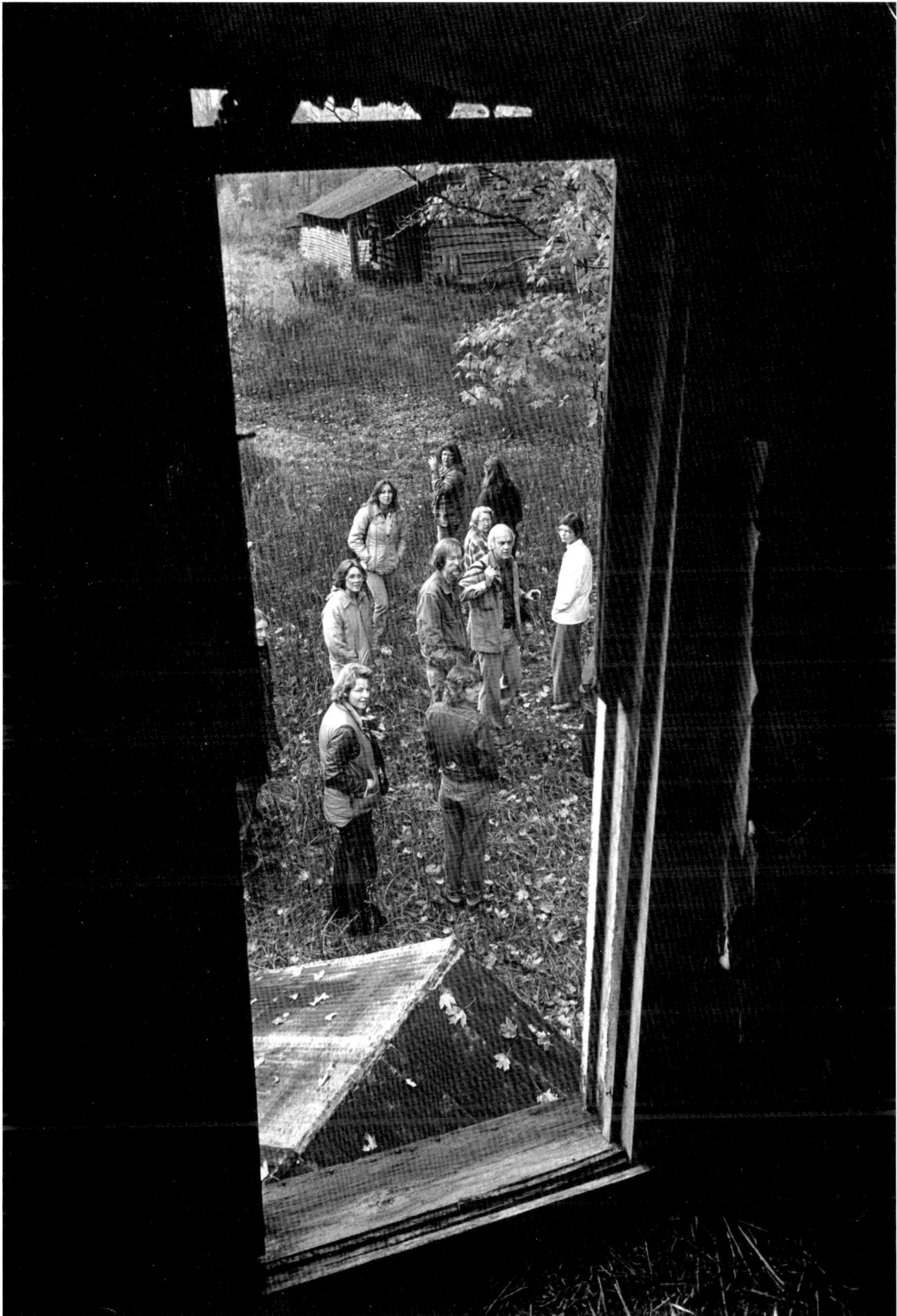

Research is not always done in libraries and archives. Lynwood Montell [folk studies] and students investigate vernacular architecture.

. . .to rub Wilson's nose brings good luck.

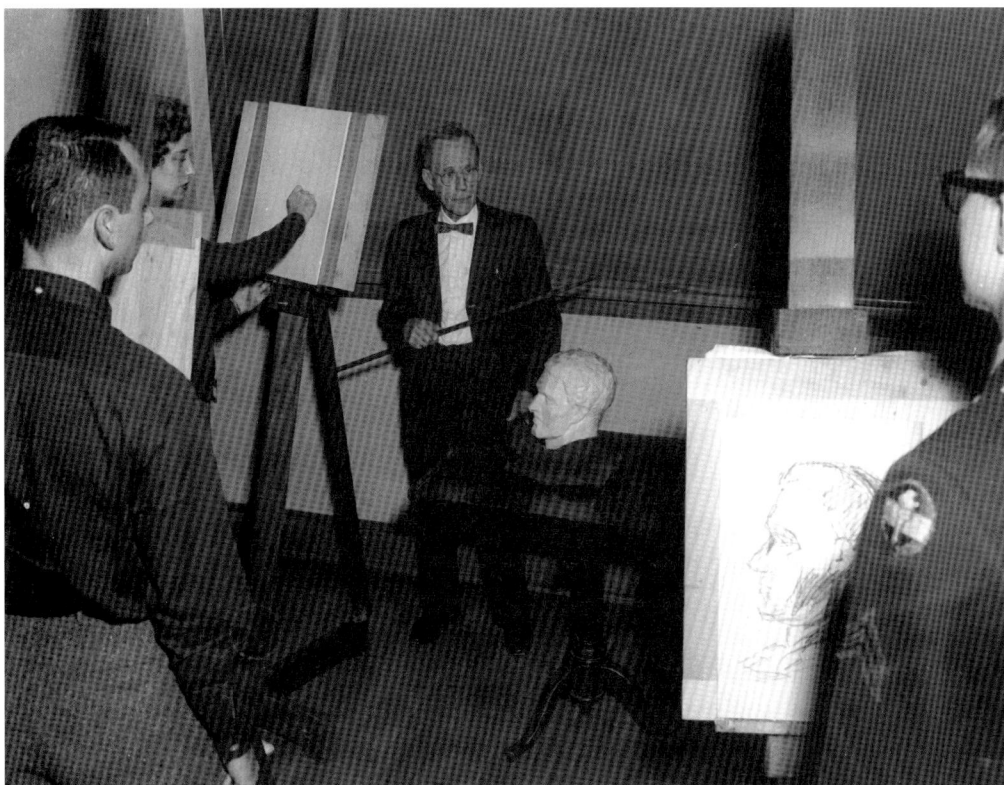

Ivan Wilson |art| painted hundreds of watercolors and oils that documented the changing local community. His portrait bust sits in a wall niche near the main entrance to the Fine Arts Center. Tradition says that to rub Wilson's nose brings good luck.

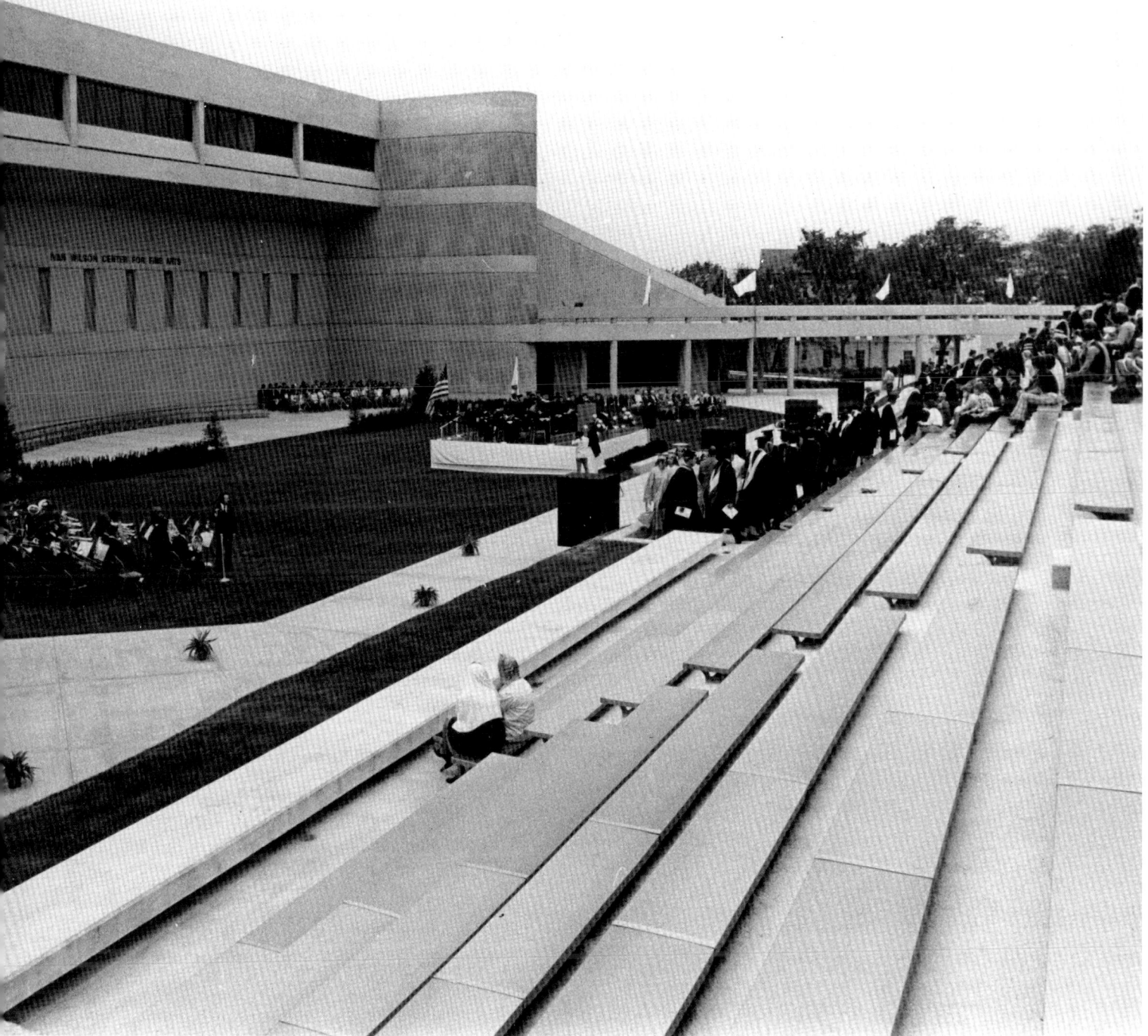

Highlights of the 1973 dedication of the Ivan Wilson Fine Arts Center featured the Cincinnati Ballet, a performance by pianist Van Cliburn, and a concert by the Roger Wagner Chorale.

They had never fought a duel.

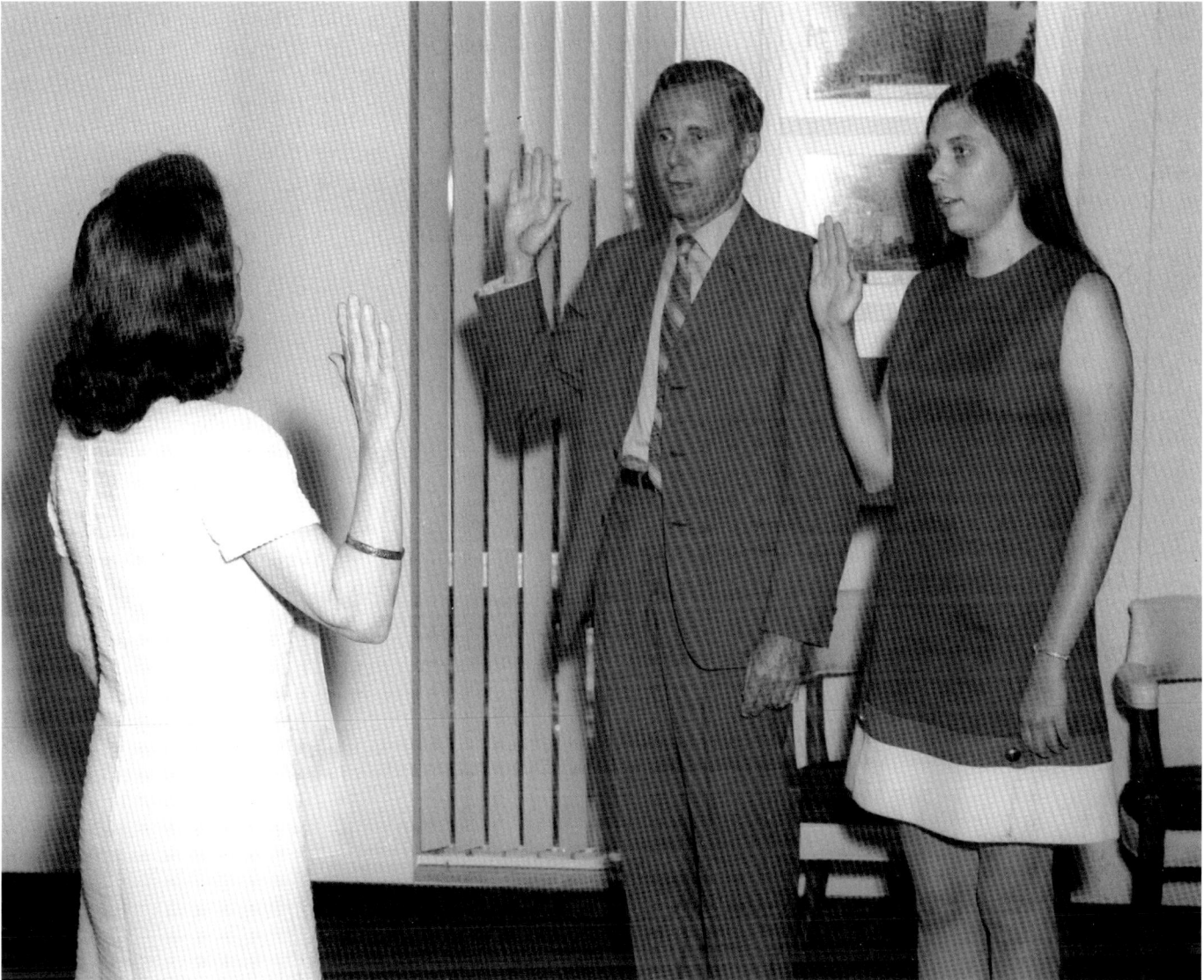

Student and faculty regents joined the university's governing board in 1968. In 1971 Lowell Harrison [history] and Linda Jones, the first female student regent, swore that they had never fought a duel, a requirement for holding public office in Kentucky. Neither could vote!

The Rodes-Helm Lecture Series

Not all learning is for academic credit. The Rodes-Helm Lecture Series has brought impressive names to campus, including editor William Buckley, newsman David Brinkley and British MP Bernadette Devlin. In 1967 Margie Helm [librarian] and Vice President Raymond Cravens [government] enjoyed listening to author Pearl Buck.

Antiwar

In the 1960s and 70s the nation witnessed hundreds of antiwar protests and civil rights demonstrations. In October 1969, twelve hundred students filled Western's old stadium for a five-hour Vietnam War Moratorium led by Lerond Curry [history].

Peaceful demonstrations

Associated Student Government and its elected members served as a safety valve, and through it demands, requests and opinions were peacefully channeled to the administration.

In the early 1970s more than 250 African American students conducted a peaceful sit-in at the Wetherby Administration Building. Meeting with President Downing, they demanded greater representation on the cheerleading squad and in other campus groups. Although students protested and held rallies, Western did not witness the destructive turmoil and unrest that plagued other campuses.

The Honors Colloquium began in 1962 and nine years later gained its first full-time director. Professors and students from a variety of disciplines plan the program's course of study. L–R: James Baker [history], David Anderson, Louella Fong [home economics], Paul Corts [speech], Jim Wayne Miller [German].

The Fulbright Scholar Program granted Carlton Jackson [history] the university's first Fulbright and shortly thereafter undergraduates began to receive student awards. Raymond Cravens [government] congratulates Ron Cameron, a 1972 Fulbright recipient

Western Kentucky University, 1975. By the mid-1970s Western's second big building era had ended.

Awards Day has traditionally highlighted WKU's academic year. In 1974 President Downing recognized the achievements of Gary Ransdell.

RECENT DECADES

During the last quarter-century, Western Kentucky University has witnessed a significant gain in enrollment. More students have necessitated additional faculty and staff and new and/or renovated residence halls, classrooms and auxiliary buildings. The means by which the university reaches students has also changed. Branch campuses, interactive television classes and on-line courses indicate the university's interest in making education accessible to a wider segment of the population. New majors, special emphasis studies, certificate programs and joint doctorate affiliations also reflect progress.

Students, faculty and staff have played a more active role in campus affairs through governance groups, such as the Student Government Association, Faculty Senate, the University Senate, and Staff Council. Diversity contributes to the success of every segment of the university. Non-traditional students make up an increasingly larger percentage of the enrollment. Once a regional school, Western attracts people from every state as well as from more than sixty foreign nations. A variety of departments offer studies abroad. Western prepares students to be productive citizens in a global society and to understand the need for life-long learning.

But there is also a lighter side to university life. Although tempered in recent years, campus shenanigans still include streaking, hazing and mooning. Occasionally President Cherry's statue sports feminine finery, toilet paper sometimes decorates trees and shrubs, underground faculty evaluations pop up periodically, and parking permits remain mere hunting licenses. When former students are asked about their time on the Hill, they recall the friendliness, warmth, and genuine concern the faculty and staff showed them; the beauty of the campus; and the lifelong friendships they developed while living in Bowling Green. Sometimes a t-shirt can tell it all. Worn on campus by a pre-med major, it read: "I did not come to college to get a husband, I came to find my bridesmaids."

Seven presidents have led Western during the last quarter-century: Dero Downing [1969–1979], John D. Minton [1979], Donald W. Zacharias [1979–1985], Kern Alexander [1986–1988], Thomas C. Meredith [1988–1997] and Gary Ransdell [1997–]. Interim presidents, Paul Cook [1985–1986] and Barbara Burch [1997] also provided excellent leadership during their short terms.

President Downing, well known for his interest in campus care, frequently picked up what others carelessly threw down; in doing so he instilled in students a pride and interest in keeping the campus attractive.

Photo by Lewis Gardner

81

"My books cost how much?????"

Although lines may be shorter today than in yesteryear, high costs are familiar to all college students.

Photo by Bruce Edwards

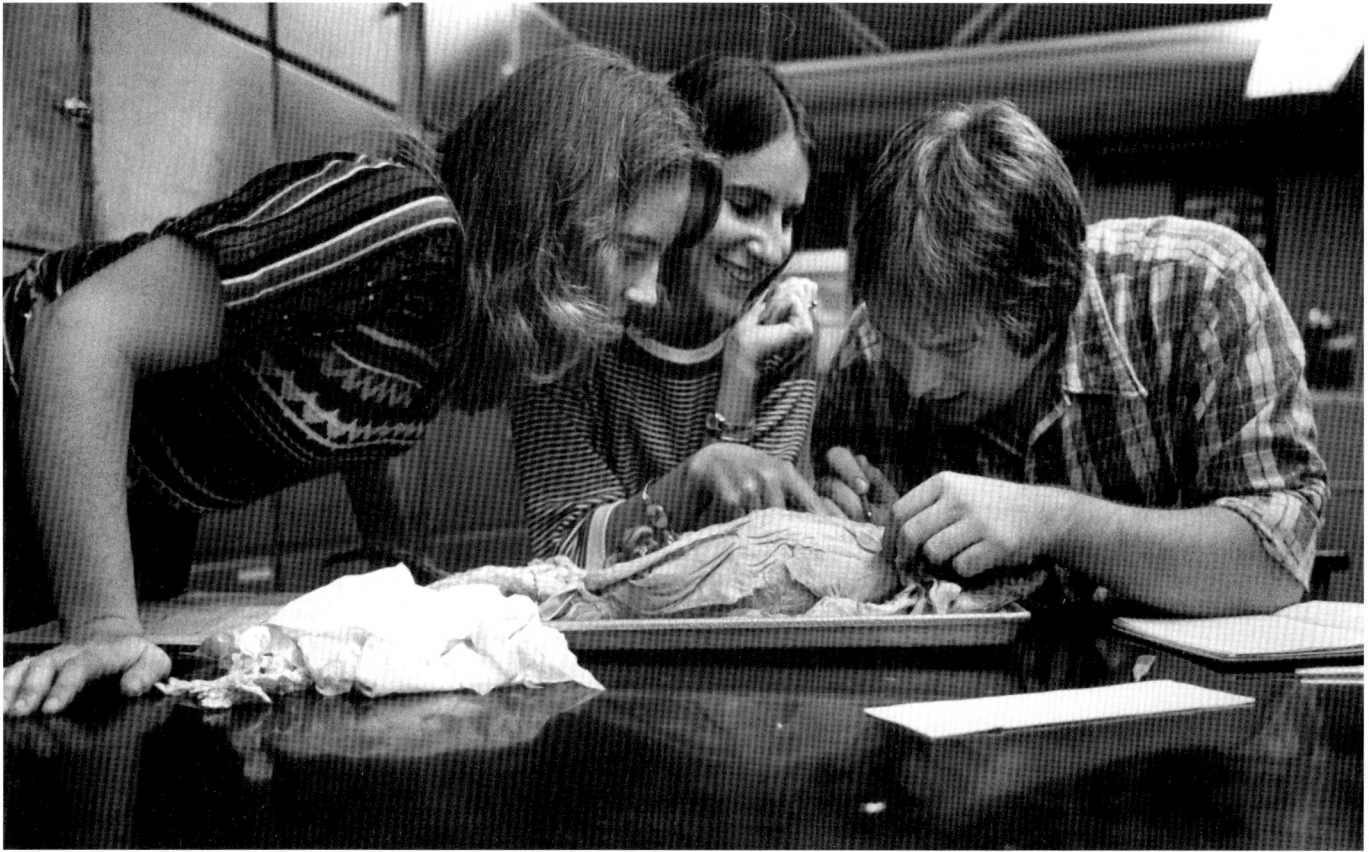

Photo by Ron Hoskins

Brenda Carter, Beverly Jackson and David Dodd dissect a cat in comparative anatomy, a required course for biology and pre-med students. Western holds an exemplary record in the acceptance rate of its graduates into professional schools.

Photo by John Rott

Entertaining for the Tri Beta (biology honor society) Ground Hog Day Picnic, Dan Skean and Larry Elliott [biology] prove that scientists have many talents.

WKYU-TV and WKYU-FM provide public broadcasting to the region as Linda Skaggs and Sherri Corum gain valuable work experience running cameras for university ball games and charitable events like the 1981 Muscular Dystrophy Telethon.

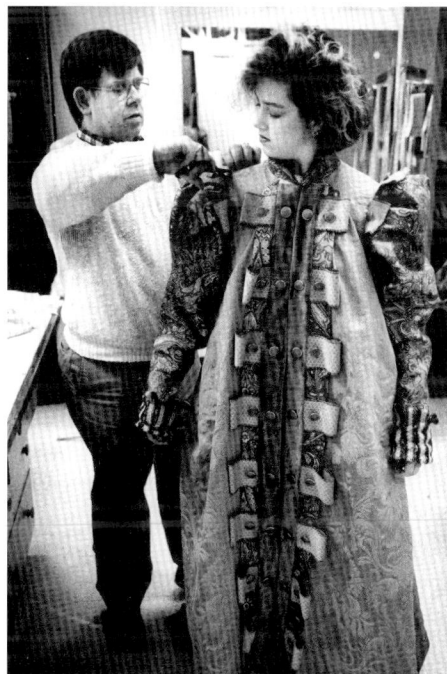

Well-designed props play an important part in the success of theatrical productions. Jackson Kesler [theatre] "directs" Paige Brooks in the design and fit of her costume.

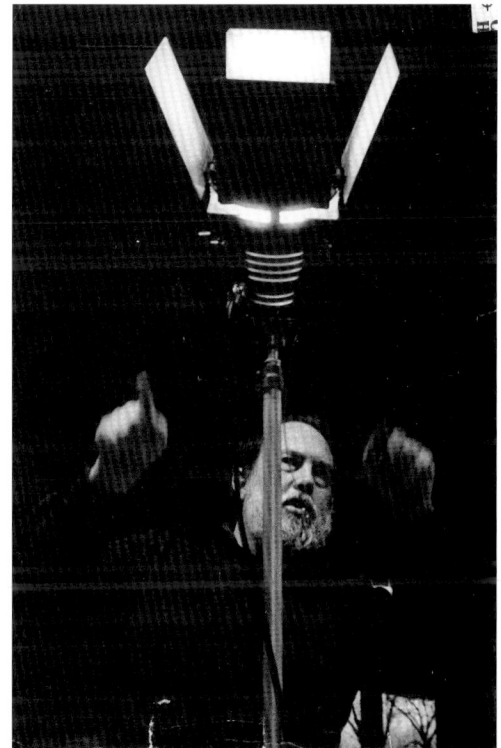

Using equipment borrowed from a local cable company, Joe Boggs [English] and a cast and crew of students filmed his play about a Peeping Tom professor and the differences between illusion, reality and the gray areas of truth.

John Minton [history] discusses university affairs with regent Hughlyne Wilson. Few administrators have served Western in more capacities than Dr. Minton: history professor, graduate dean, Athletic Committee and Title IX Chairman, Administrative Vice President, President, and Vice President of Student Affairs.

On retirement, many faculty members remain active in university-sponsored programs. Marjorie Clagett |French| often addressed groups of students about France or flowers. She and Michael Aoun discussed Alaskan plant life.

French

Photo by Rick Musacchio

"Way down to Egypt-land"

Going "way down to Egypt-land" refers to the parking lot at the southern end of campus. On several occasions, including the fall of 1982, Egypt's "Nile River" flooded the lot.

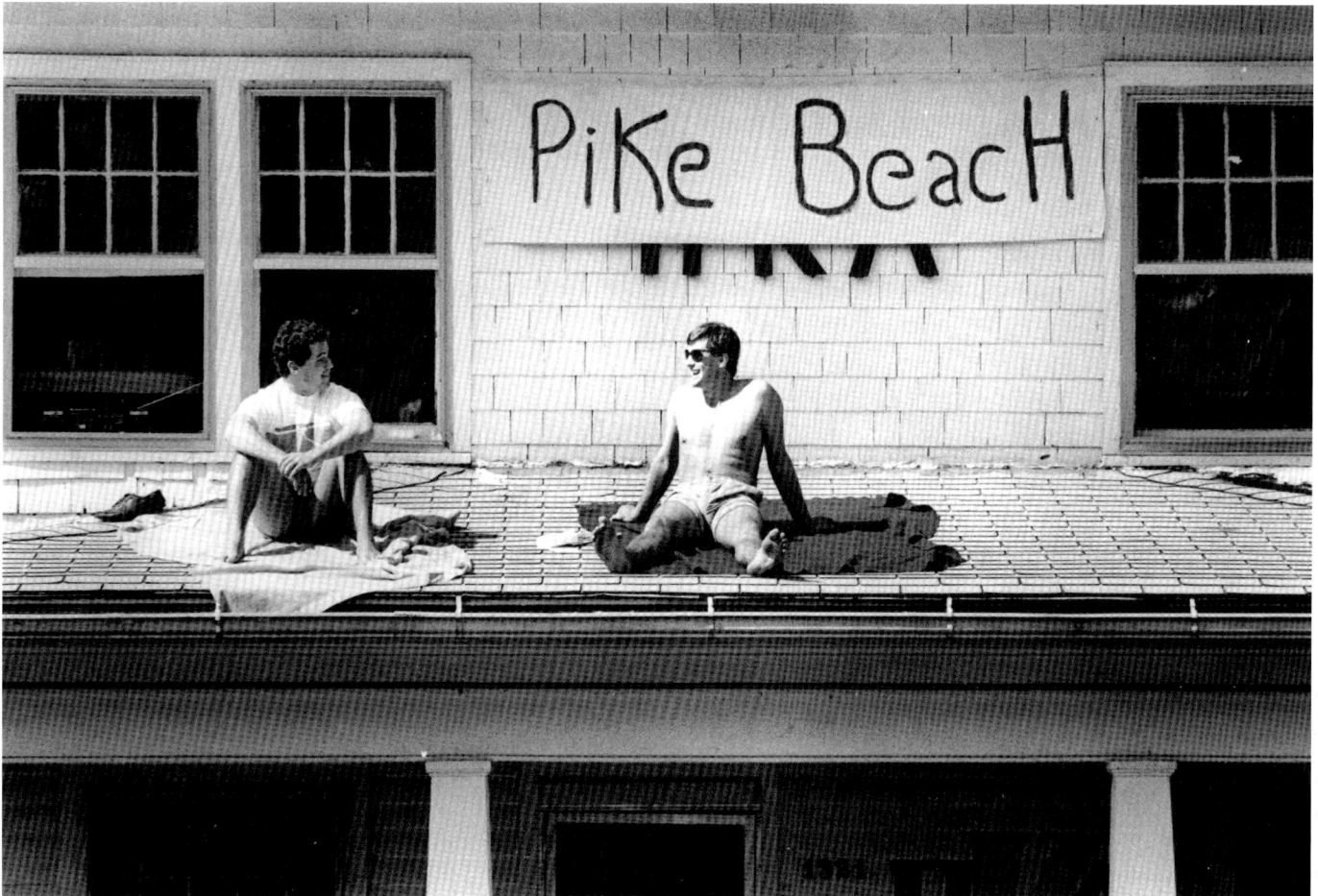

Sunbathing has always been a favorite form of relaxation for participants and passersby, whether at "Pike Beach" or in the "Valley of the Dolls," a student nickname for the quadrangle formed by Rodes-Harlin, Gilbert and McCormack halls.

"Valley of the Dolls"

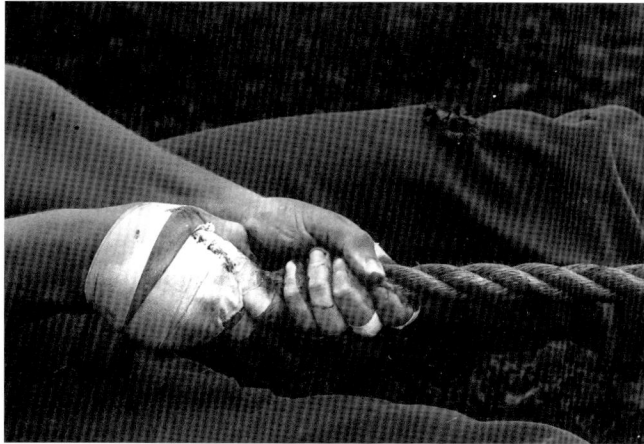

Greek Week

Spring is the time for Greek Week's competitive activities. One of the toughest—and sometimes the dirtiest—is the Tug of War.

Dr. Zacharias participated in a well-attended question-and-answer session in the Faculty House during his interview for the position of WKU president.

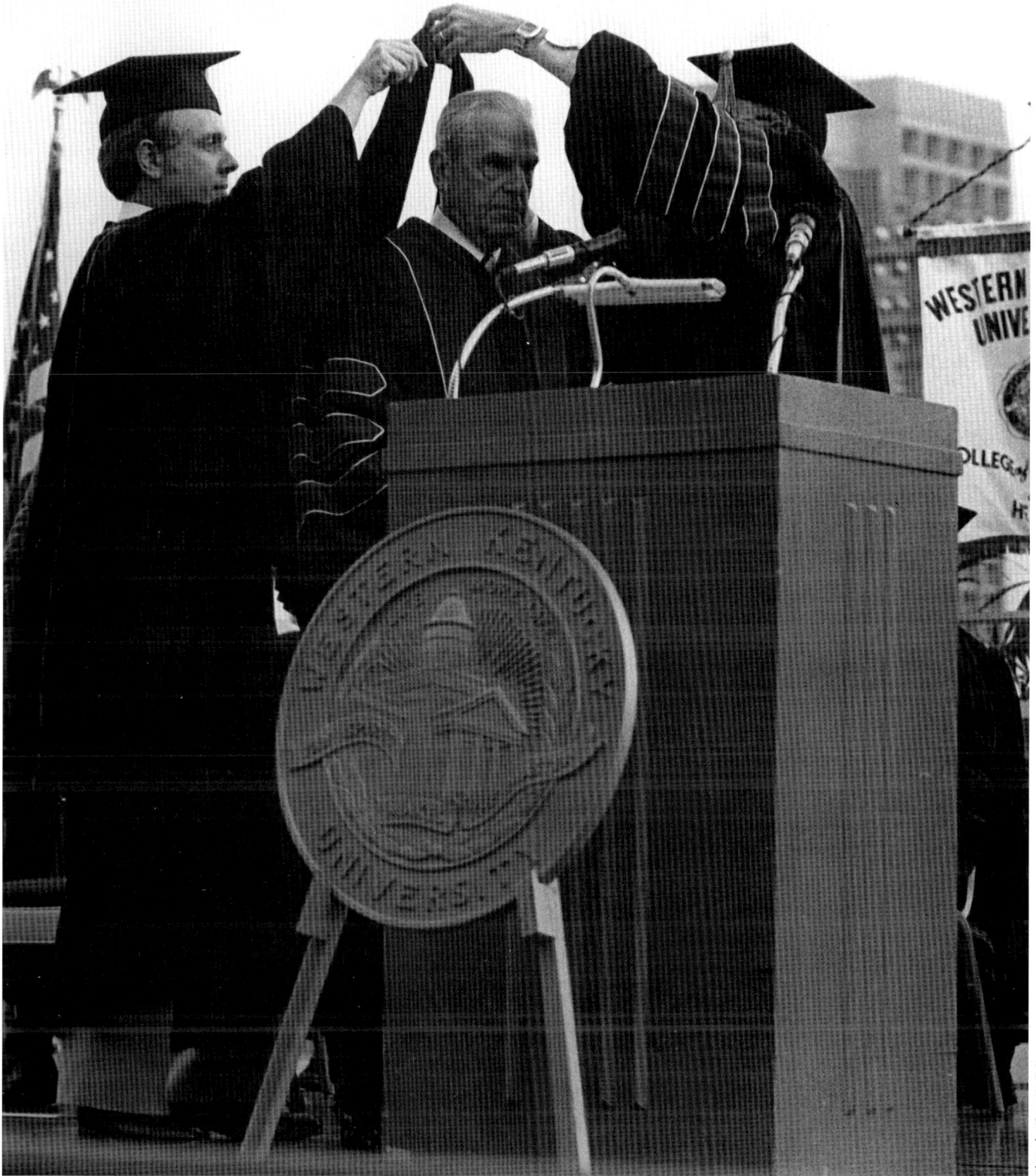

In August 1979, Vice President James Davis [geography/geology] and President Zacharias conferred Western's first honorary Doctor of Laws degree on U.S. Congressman William H. Natcher. Western adopted its official seal in 1948.

Opened in 1980 and enlarged several years later, the L.D. Brown Agricultural Exposition Center draws campus guests for concerts, trade shows, rodeos, livestock competitions and Future Farmers of America field days.

"Distance learning" classes began in the 1980s when Jack Thacker [history] and others taught through television classes delivered to Glasgow and other satellite campuses.

Photo by Margaret Shirley

Phi Alpha Theta (history) graduate students Ron Bryant, Bruce Trammell and David Dalton talk over a college bowl game question with their "warden," President Zacharias, in their successful effort to defeat the history faculty.

Photo by Bob Skipper

Over the years the university has held annual fish fries, picnics and other events to express its appreciation to faculty, staff and friends. At some of the popular "cookouts" Paul Cook [Administrative Vice President for Finance and Interim President] manned the grill.

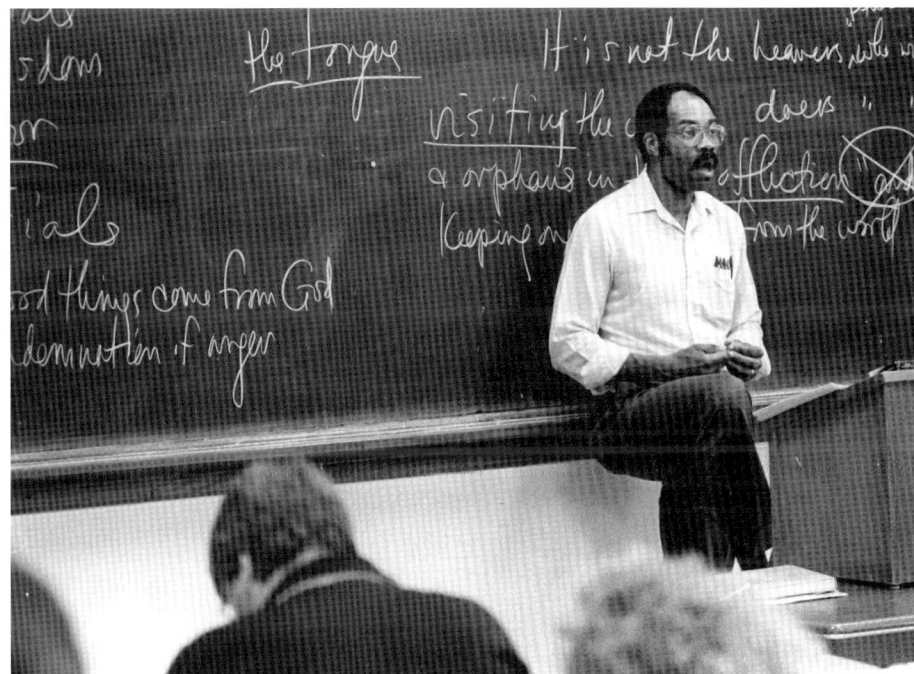

Photo by Bob Skipper

Although technology is changing, Western still offers courses presented in a traditional manner. For this class, John Long [religion] employs lecture and discussion, chalkboard and textbook.

In February 1981, President Zacharias visited the legislature to protest the state's cuts to higher education. On campus, students wearing "Back Zack" signage braved the weather to show their support of his mission.

"Back Zack"

Photo by Kim Kolarik

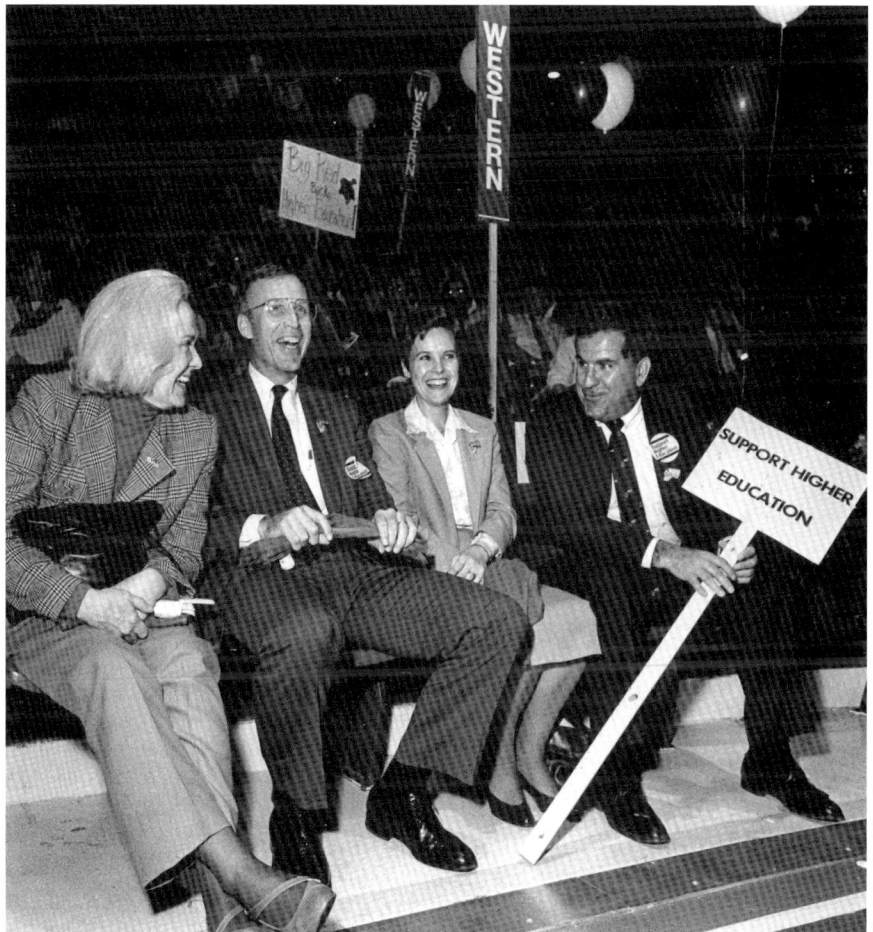

Photo by Fred Hensley

Journeys to Frankfort to seek funding never seem to cease. Shortly after he became president, Kern Alexander and regents Mary Ellen Miller [English], Patsy Judd and Joe Iracane continued the battle-for-the-budget.

Photo by Bob Skipper

Big Red has captured the hearts of Western fans. An ambassador for the university, the mascot's honors include top awards at the Universal Cheerleading Association's national competition, final four in the 1996 ESPN Battle of the Mascots and 2002 ESPN commercials.

Special Olympics bring town and gown together. In 1981 Western hosted the statewide event. Jo Verner [physical education] and Eunice Kennedy Shriver awarded the prizes.

Daily News Photo by Mark Workman

Photo by Lewis Gardner

To gain an understanding about utilizing and conserving the unique features of karst regions, Ray Tucker used Western's underground "classroom".

Learning the skills of a surveyor is crucial in a state with conflicting land claims. Engineering students have probably surveyed every inch of the campus and a sizeable portion of the town.

Biology students sometimes claim a non-traditional classroom in which they collect aquatic invertebrates for study.

With an analog computer, mechanical engineering lab assistant Bob Brown simulates landing on the moon.

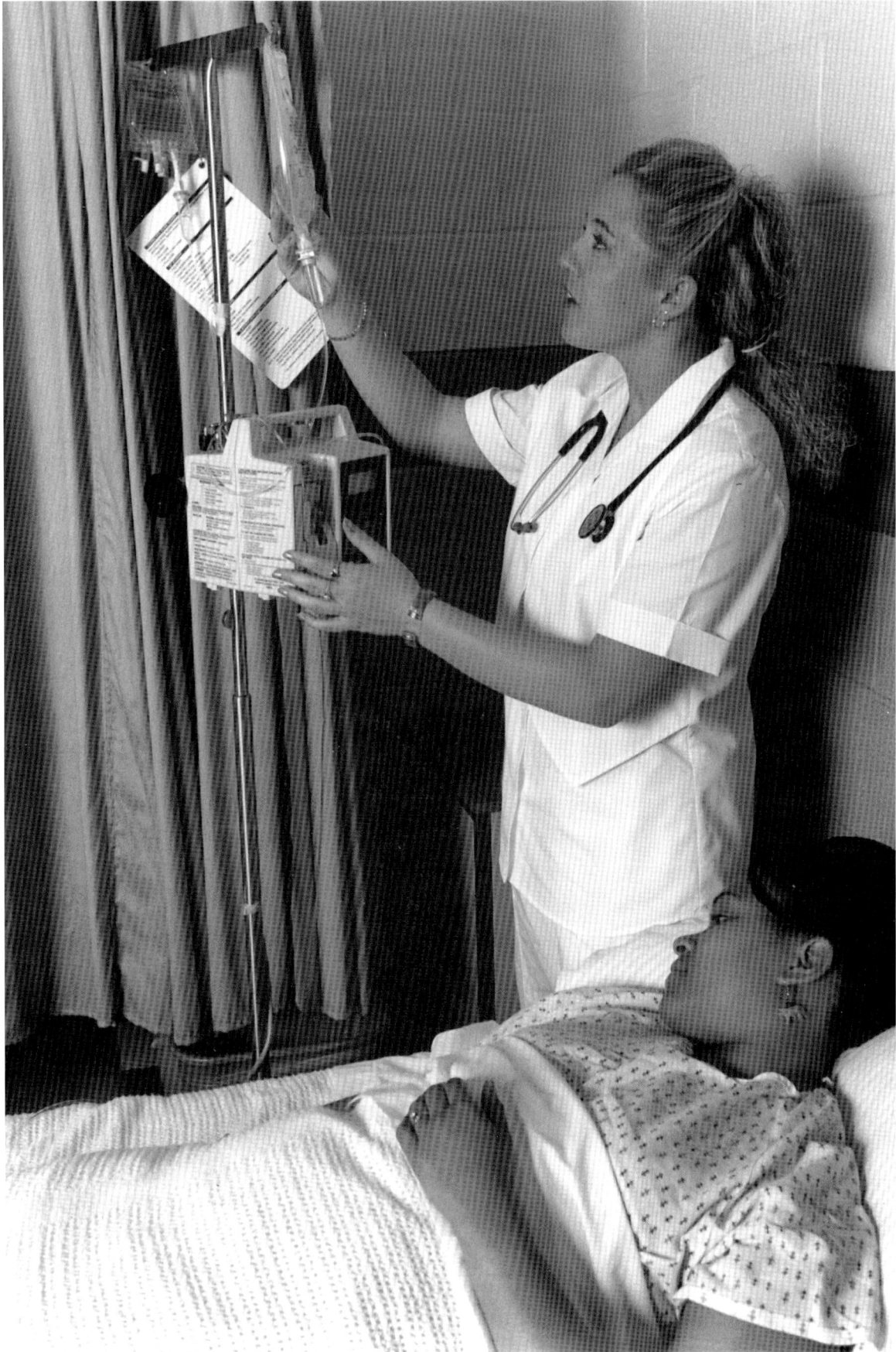

A baccalaureate degree in nursing requires 65 hours of nursing courses as well as classes in biology, psychology, chemistry, sociology and other general education classes.

Accreditation is important

Accreditation is important—and not easily obtained. To achieve it for the MBA program, Jack Stallard [information systems] and other faculty in the Gordon Ford College of Business compiled a mountain of proposals, evidence and recommendations. They succeeded.

Although often remembered for issuing parking tickets, public safety officers Hugh Heater (pictured here helping a student replace her license plate) and his colleagues ensure the safety and quality of campus life.

Diligence and Care

The beauty of Western's campus results from the diligence and care given by L. J. Reagan and his Facilities Management colleagues.

Photo by Sheryl Hagan-Booth

Mary Taylor Cowles led the Lady Toppers to a Sun Belt Tournament title and was named Sun Belt Conference Coach-of-the-Year—all in her first year as coach!

During his 15 years as coach of women's basketball, Paul Sanderford and his team compiled a 365–120 record, competed in 12 NCAA tournaments, and appeared in the Final Four three times and the Women's NIT in two additional seasons.

Intramural football teams with creative names abound and local businesses often supply the jerseys. L–R: Don Sullivan, Alfred Thompson, Charlie Cowherd, and Allen DeWeese.

They can swim "faster than anyone" and championship coach Bill Powell and his swimmers hold an impressive array of awards to prove it.

Western's baseball program has produced 15 All-Americans. In 2005 Coach Joel Murrie won his 800th victory.

Elaborately decorated residence halls and sorority/fraternity houses are an important part of homecoming festivities.

University departments and social organizations join in Homecoming's Festival of Friends with tents on the south lawn. Tailgating has become popular for all home football games.

To build a beautiful float requires hours of labor, miles of chicken wire and tons of crepe paper, paper napkins and toilet paper. L–R: Sandy Pierce, Eva Sutton and Carol Ann Young.

As part of the 1991 President for a Day raffle, President Meredith and a student traded places and both undoubtedly obtained important new perspectives about the university.

The Raymond B. Preston Health and Activities Center opened in 1992. To students and faculty the center offers access to large gyms, a jogging skyway, 9 racquetball courts, 2 weight training rooms, aerobic dance area, a fitness room, 25-meter pool and performance lab.

In the 1990s Western built two residence halls for women. Divided into suites rather than rooms, the new structures offered amenities not available elsewhere on campus. "Someone actually took time to think about what the students wanted," surmised one of its residents. Named for former presidents, Meredith Hall and "Zack's Shack" are "suite places to live."

Photo by Alan Warren

To help address the parking dilemma, the university instituted a shuttle service. One route encircles the main campus and the other connects it and south campus to a large parking lot near the Preston Sports Complex on Campbell Lane. In 2004 construction began on a second parking structure.

Expand their horizons

Photo by Leslie Page

Photo by Sheryl Hagan-Booth

The Bowling Green Community College is the fastest growing portion of the university. Housed with the Carroll Knicely Conference Center on Nashville Road, its open admission policy encourages students of every age to expand their horizons.

The annual phone-a-thon helps the university stay in touch with faculty, students and alumni and thus fosters its continued growth. With Big Red are L–R: Luther Hughes [agriculture], Joann Albers [journalism], Sharon Lee, Kim Hoffman, Amos Gott.

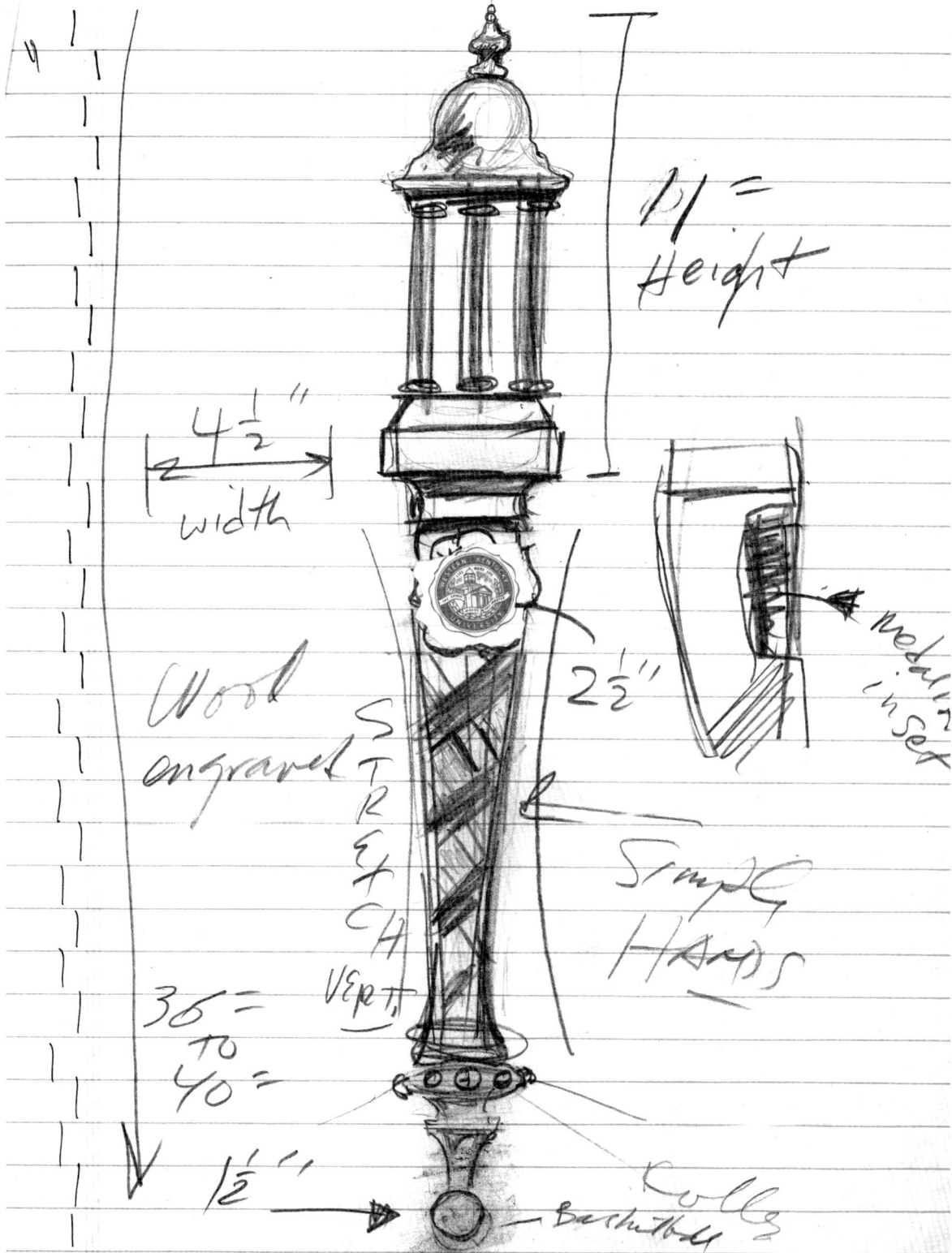

Designed by John Warren Oakes (art), crafted by Terry Leeper (industrial technology) and created for formal university celebrations, the mace is carried by the most senior member of the faculty at the head of academic processions. The ancient symbol of authority made its debut at the May 1998 inauguration of President Gary Ransdell.

President Ransdell breaks ground for a second parking structure as he "moves" the university forward. As Western begins its second hundred years, it completes a century of amazing growth and embarks on another era of construction, expansion and progress.

INTO THE TWENTY-FIRST CENTURY

Western's campus continues to "blossom" during the 21st century. Beautifully kept grounds, stately shade trees and colorful flower gardens enhance new and established structures. Two new classroom buildings, renovated dorms, an enlarged student center, improved athletic facilities and another parking structure have changed the Western landscape. And more construction is scheduled. The 2005 Kentucky legislature approved the university's request for funds to renovate Science and Technology Hall (the 1925 Training School) and the Thompson Complex Central Wing; to replace Thompson North Wing with a new structure and to build a campus health center. Additional changes are also slated for the South Campus and for the Center for Research and Development. The US Congressional budget also approved a USDA Research Lab. WKU is indeed a school on the move!

"I don't know Herb, it just doesn't seem like the same ole place!

All residence halls have been remodeled, rewired and air-conditioned and are protected with smoke detectors and sprinkler systems. Virginia Garrett Avenue, once a cut-through between Big Red Way and Normal Drive, now serves as an attractive walkway and green space linking North, South, East and West halls (renamed Northeast and Southwest halls).

The 125-foot Guthrie Tower, a salute to those who served this nation, is a gathering place for students and the site of the Freshman Convocation. Russ Faxon's life-size statue of Robert Guthrie, killed during the Korean War, stands near the tower. Mass Media and Technology Hall is on the far side of the tower.

Completed in 2003 Mass Media
and Technology Hall offers a
computer lab that is open
around the clock and has state-
of-the-art laser printers and
other equipment. The building
also boasts a large auditorium
and the Cornelius A. Martin
Regents Room.

2003

At the groundbreaking ceremony for the Complex for Engineering and Biological Sciences, a miniature Big Red robot made by engineering students lifted the first shovel of dirt. Opened in the 2004–05 academic year, the building houses biology labs, and a conference room, laboratory, and design and project centers for civil, electrical and mechanical engineering.

"Diddle Do-Over"

Photo by Sheryl Hagan-Booth

In the early months of the 21st century the basketball arena received what the *Herald* labeled a "Diddle Do-Over." Next to the renovated arena, the university constructed a second parking structure and built additions that nearly double the size of DUC. Big Red Way also received a new look—and two new names, College Heights Boulevard and Avenue of Champions.

In the McConnell Integrated Applications Laboratory, Mary Elizabeth Baker demonstrates her steam engine for Kevin Schmaltz [engineering] and Robert Choate [engineering].

Western offers graduate and undergraduate courses through its extended campus programs at Glasgow, Owensboro and Elizabethtown. Local, state and national dignitaries helped cut the ribbon at the dedication of Western's new South Regional Post-Secondary Education Center at Glasgow. L–R: Matt Gumm, Charles Honeycutt, Jody Richards, Steve Nunn, Juanita Bayless, Sandra Appling, Richie Sanders, Kristen Bale, Tommy Gumm.

From the new Van Meter overlook one has a breathtaking view of the campus and the Kentucky countryside.

The Kentucky Academy of Mathematics and Science, a residential program for high school juniors and seniors, will be housed in Schneider Hall. The 1929 structure offers handsome architectural details.

Photo by David Frank

Photo by Sheryl Hagan-Booth

In 2003 Western alumni Nappy Roots presented their first gold record to the university and President Ransdell.

127

Accolades

Western boasts many award winning programs. The forensic team may be the university's oldest student organization. Founded in 1906, its current members (all of whom have 3.35–4.0 GPAs) represent nearly every discipline. Under Judy Woodring's direction, the team has repeatedly garnered state, national and international accolades. With Woodring are students: Justin Cress, Jordan Wadlington, Doug Mory, Jennifer Purcell, Stacy Bernaugh, Nicole Hawk, Hannah Reliford, Joelle Perry, Reagan Gibson, Joe Day and Alex Rogers.

Year after year Western's journalism department has been proclaimed the nation's number one by Hearst Publishers. Consequently it draws top students from across the country. The *College Heights Herald* also continues to rack up awards as it informs and entertains its readers.

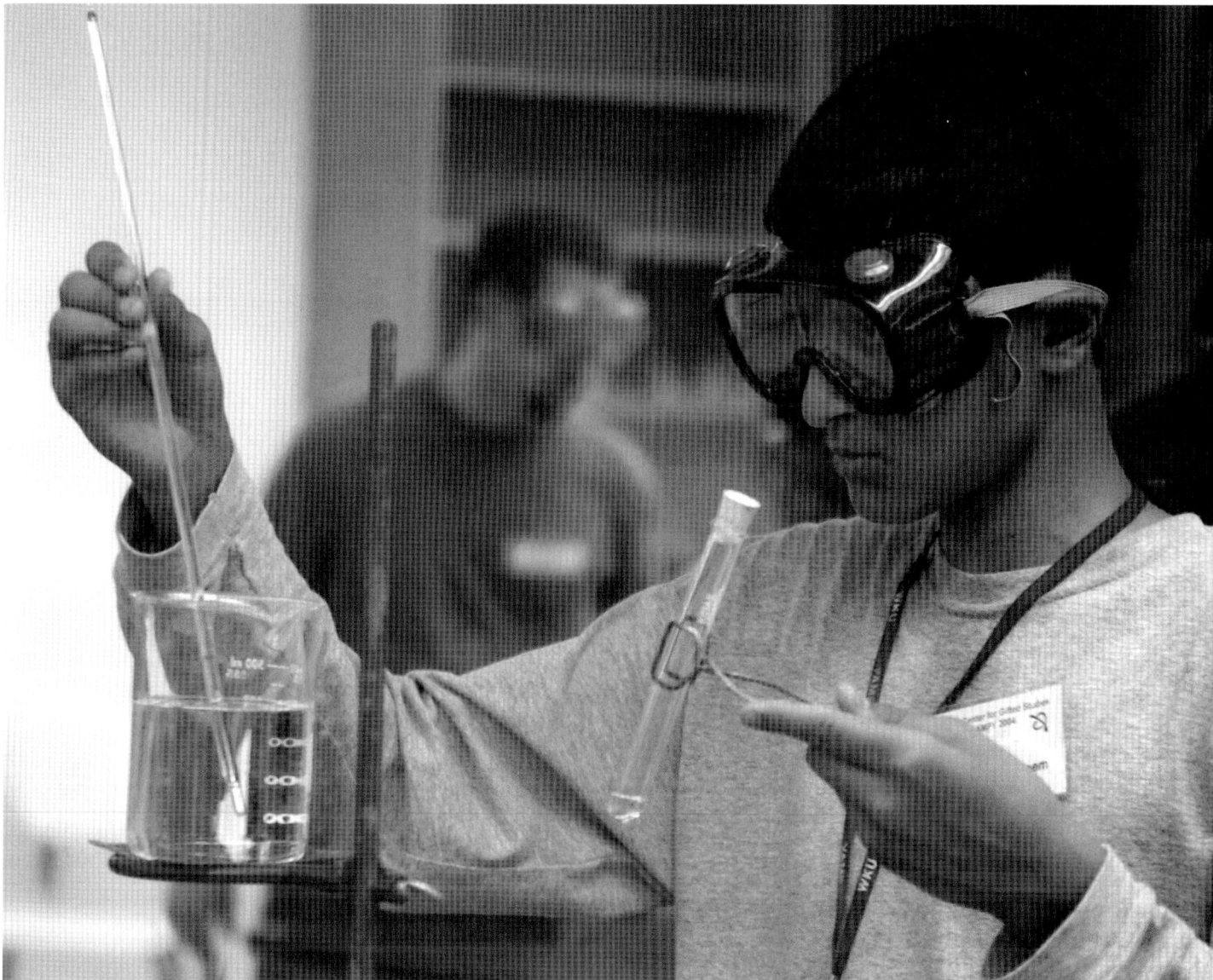

Photo by Sheryl Hagan-Booth

Some of Western's award-winning programs are for future college students. The university's Center for Gifted Studies program offers Saturday and summer "Vampy" classes for Verbally and Mathematically Precocious Youths—like this budding chemist. Julia Roberts [education] heads the program.

VAMPY

In 2002 the Hilltoppers finished their football season as the NCAA Division
I-AA National Champions.

Artist Proof

133

VE Day

To help Russia celebrate the 60th anniversary of VE Day, the 80-member Wind Ensemble "tooted Western's horn" at concerts in St. Petersburg and Moscow. They pose here in front of the former Winter Palace of the Czars, now the Hermitage Museum.

Sculptor Russ Faxon's statue of Coach E.A. Diddle was made for and dedicated during the celebration of Western's centennial.

Photo by Sheryl Hagan-Booth

Western's Centennial

Julie Ransdell, Gordon and Glenda Ford, Richard Frock and other guests enjoy the recent President's Circle Gala, a salute to generous donors. During the 1998-2003 Investing in the Spirit campaign, and with the support of students, faculty, alumni and friends, the university raised more than $102 million.

President's Circle Gala

Each graduation processional includes flags of all the nations represented by the
new graduates.

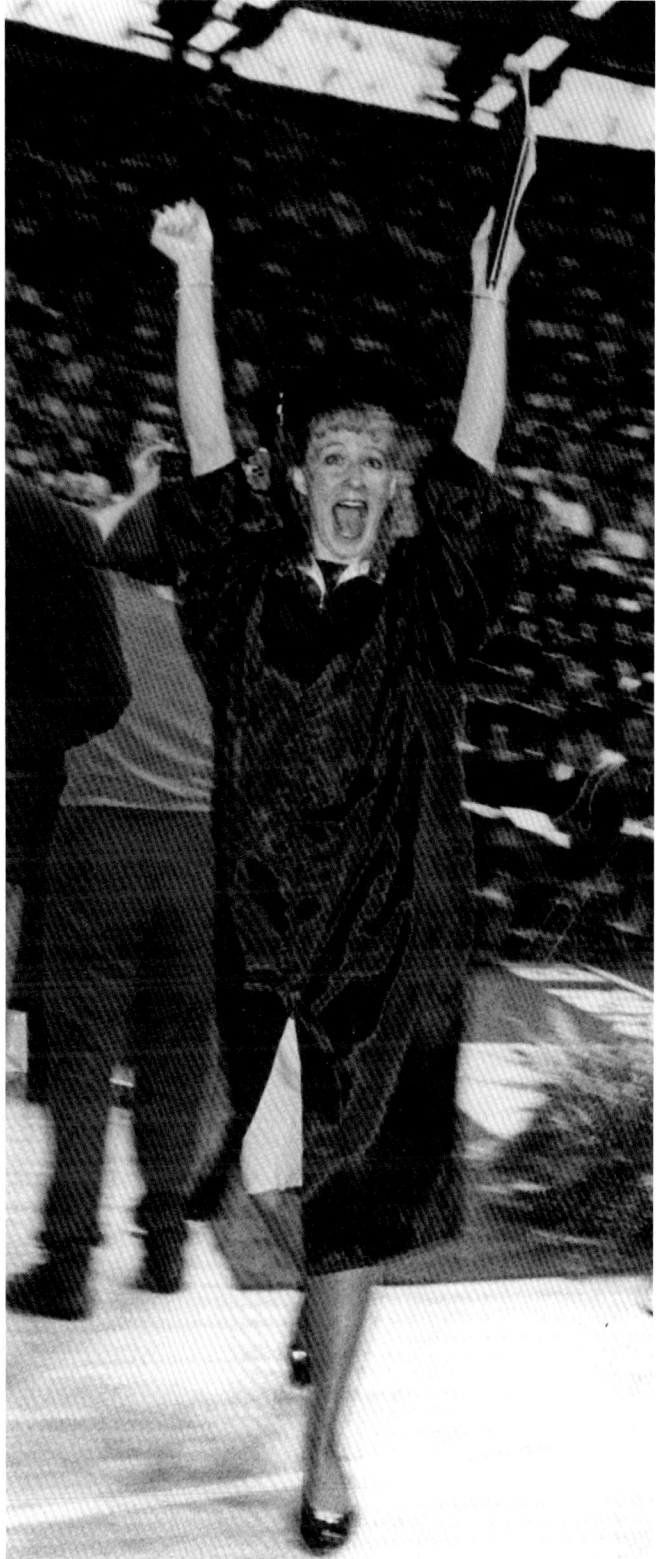

Commencement is—and certainly should be—every student's dream. A new graduate illustrates the joy of academic achievement.

Photo by Kurt L. Vinson